Juggling Elephants?

Juggling Elehants?

Be The Ringmaster of
Your Work and Life

(peanuts not included)

Jones Loflin & Todd Musig

ELUCIDATE
PUBLISHING

Salt Lake City, Utah

Dedicated to our families

and to those who struggle with

"getting it all done."

For further information on *Juggling Elephants?* products and services:
1-800-853-4676 • www.jugglingelephants.com

Book and Cover Design by Tom Hewitson

The circus is a change of pace—

beauty against our daily ugliness,

excitement against our boredom.

Every man, woman and child

comes from the circus refreshed

and renewed and ready to survive!

— John Steinbeck

Table of Contents

Before
the Story

Setting Up the Tent

Mark smiled. His division was experiencing another successful quarter. While his peers thought they could identify the reasons for Mark's achievements, only Mark knew the *real* secret behind both his individual and his team's success.

Mark's successes were familiar to many in the organization. On more than one occasion, he had been selected to speak to a group of people or talk one-on-one with employees who felt overwhelmed or disengaged.

Success was evident in areas of his life outside of work, also. While he no longer had his schoolboy physique, he was still the picture of health. Friends remarked that he had the energy of someone half his age.

He and Lisa had raised three wonderful children. Jackie was married and working in a large company. Evan was completing his degree and would soon be looking for a job. Brian had started his own business after high school. Through it all, he and Lisa remained each other's biggest fan and were closer than ever.

The buzz of the phone interrupted his reflection.

"You have a visitor, Mark," his assistant said.

"Who is it?" he asked.

"It's a surprise."

"Come on, Carol," Mark replied. "Just tell me who it is."

"I am not telling you," Carol quipped, "and that's final. If you want to know who it is, you'll have to come out and see for yourself!"

Half aggravated and half curious, he went to the door and opened it. There stood his daughter Jackie.

"Surprised?" she asked as they hugged.

"That's an understatement!" Mark made a face at Carol, led Jackie into his office and closed the door.

"Have a seat. This *is* a wonderful surprise. What brings you here?" Mark asked.

"Officially," Jackie began, "I had a meeting here in town this morning, and we finished up a little while ago. Unofficially, I came to see *you*."

Jackie's mood quickly became more serious.

"I am struggling with something, and I need your help."

Mark prepared himself for the worst. He feared it might be related to her marriage, although he had not seen any red flags. He took a deep breath and hesitantly asked, "So what's going on?"

"Everything!" she blurted out. "I love my job, but I just can't seem to keep up. I thought the other two people in my department would make things easier, but I'm beginning to think they don't care *what* happens in the company.

"Brett is a very supportive husband, but he's busy with his own job. We are almost too accepting of our lack of time together, and that worries me. We just seem to be dividing and conquering all the time, jumping from one thing to another. Sometimes none of it makes sense.

"To complicate things further," Jackie continued, "Brett and I are beginning to talk about starting a family. I don't have a clue how I could be a decent parent with my crazy life!"

"Sounds pretty serious, honey. How are you holding up?" Mark asked.

"I'm getting by," Jackie replied. "I go to work and do the best I can, but I just wish I had a moment for myself now and then."

"So how can I help?" Mark asked.

"I'm not sure you realize it, Dad, but I've watched you more than you will ever know," Jackie answered.

"Beginning my own career and experiencing the struggles of keeping it all together, I often reflect on how you and Mom handle things."

"What do you mean?" Mark asked.

"For instance," Jackie replied, "The way you always seem to know the most important thing to do at any given moment. You and Mom have accomplished so much, yet I hardly ever saw you struggle like I do. I just can't figure out what's wrong with me. Not to mention the mess that I have going on at work. All this stress is causing me to seriously think about looking for another job."

Mark patted Jackie's hand. "First of all," he began, "I know that you have everything it takes to lead a full and rewarding life. I have no doubt that you can succeed in your current position.

"Second, I struggled more than you will ever know with many of the same life challenges. Your mother did, too. Oh, the stories we could tell you. We still have moments of frustration now, but it is easier because of where we are in our careers and our personal lives.

"What made the difference for us was discovering how to focus our time and energy on the things that are most important to us. We started using the process at work and later used it in other areas of our lives.

"In fact, I have *you* to thank," Mark added.

"Me?" Jackie replied.

"Yes, when you were about five years old, you helped me get my act together," Mark said.

"How?" Jackie quipped. "And if it's so helpful, why haven't you or Mom shared it with me?"

Mark took a deep breath and said, "Jackie, you and I are a lot alike. There was a time when I thought I had all the answers. When I started feeling overwhelmed at work, I questioned whether I could be successful.

"I discovered that I needed to find a way to get the right things done at the right time," he continued. "I knew that if I didn't, it could affect not only my performance at work, but also my relationship with you and your Mom as well as my own personal well-being. It was around that same time that your mom and I took you to the circus."

"The circus?" Jackie said incredulously. "You have got to be kidding. You're going to tell me that the circus will help me with life? No offense, Dad, but I think I'm a little old for clowns and elephants."

Mark smiled. "Let me ask you a question," he said. "When you are frustrated or feel like you can't focus or get things done at work, does it seem like you're trying to juggle elephants?"

Jackie paused for a moment. "I never thought about it that way, but yes," she answered with a weak smile. "That's a pretty good visual for how I feel. It just seems like getting everything done is an impossible task."

"How long can you stay?" Mark asked.

"I have a couple of hours before I need to head home," Jackie answered. "Why?"

Mark stood up and walked behind his desk. He opened a drawer and took out a notebook lying next to a tattered circus program.

"Unfortunately, I have a meeting in a few minutes that I cannot miss. It should take about an hour. I do want to talk with you more about your frustrations.

"While I'm gone, I want you to read something," Mark said. "Over the years, several people have asked me to share my insights. Some even encouraged me to write a book. I laughed, because I certainly don't consider myself to be a self-help guru. Several years ago, though, I did turn my thoughts into a story, thinking I might do something with it.

"When I get back from my meeting, let's talk about what you've read. Who knows, maybe something in it will help."

"OK, Dad," Jackie said as she took the notebook from him. "I still think you're nuts, but I'll give it a read."

Mark gave Jackie a quick hug and headed off to his meeting. She settled into the chair and began reading the story.

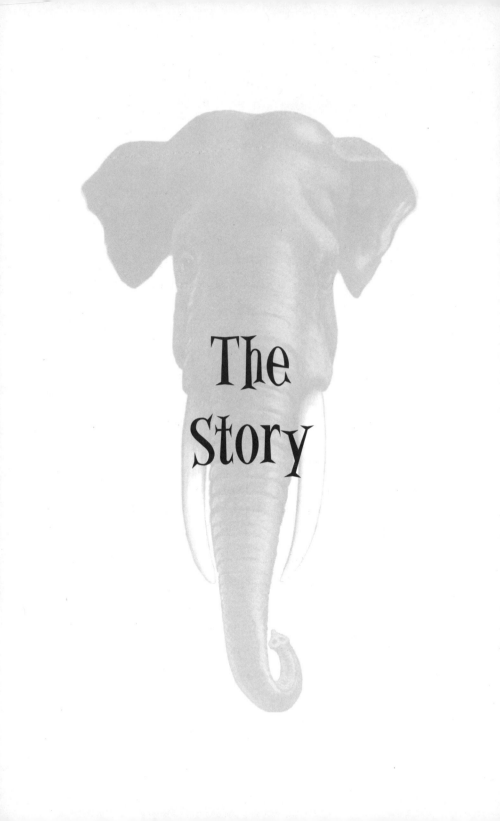

The
Story

Tickets, Please!

Mark looked at his to-do list and sighed. His day was filled with meetings, responding to messages, checking on projects and taking care of the usual administrative tasks. He knew the rest of his time would be filled with mini-crises and other fires to put out.

His evening wasn't lining up to be much better. Errands after work and a long list of unfinished projects awaited him. "Not exactly a life-changing day," he thought.

Before tackling his first task, Mark glanced longingly out the office window. He had been relatively successful to this point and now was a manager in a fast-growing organization. The workload seemed to grow from demanding to overwhelming at times, and Mark always felt like his next project needed to be more successful than the last.

Keeping himself and his staff focused, energized and productive was one of his greatest hurdles, and he knew the challenge would not get any easier with the changing economy.

Normally, he would welcome such challenges, but lately he lacked the mental and physical energy to fully engage in his tasks. In fact, his inability to focus on work was becoming a major concern. He wondered how he could expect to accomplish his professional goals if he couldn't work effectively at his current level of responsibility.

Taking a deep breath, he thought about another source of dissatisfaction: his personal life. His new position at the company required more of his time, so exercise had been put aside.

Mark had allowed his work schedule to turn breakfast and lunch into a "grab-and-go" routine of convenience foods that gave quick relief from hunger but were not helping his waistline or ability to maintain consistent energy levels.

Having had no down time in many months, Mark thought about how much he missed getting away from it all. He enjoyed hiking, fishing and spending time at the beach. These activities brought sanity into his life; the fresh air, simple sounds and relaxed pace revitalized him.

Mark thought of something else he missed: running. He had been an avid cross-country runner in high school and continued running 5k races in college. His dream was to run a marathon, but career, marriage and parenthood demands had eliminated running from his routine. "The only running I do now," he thought, "is chasing Jackie around the house."

Mark glanced at the picture of the two most important people in his life: his wife, Lisa, and their daughter, Jackie. Lisa had always been his greatest source of support, and he was her biggest fan. Oh, the things they had been through together. Lisa had worked to support the family while he completed his graduate degree. Mark had spent countless weekends and nights remodeling their home a few years ago. Even now, the smell of fresh paint made him anxious because he knew several home improvement projects were still unfinished.

Jackie, with her big smile and blue eyes, could light up his life like nothing else. The tea parties, "you can't catch me" games and pretending to be her horse were priceless mental treasures. His smile dropped as he thought of how much he missed those daddy-daughter moments.

Lisa was always good at recognizing when she and Mark needed some time together and was quick to suggest a walk or dinner out. Jackie, however, wasn't always as persistent, and he regretted missed opportunities to spend time with her.

"The circus!" he thought. Mark spun his chair around and looked at the date. In his haste to get his daily plan together, he had neglected one very critical item.

Several weeks ago, in an attempt to do better in his relationship with Jackie, he had agreed to take the family to the circus. Looking at his packed schedule, he realized it would be almost impossible to leave work early and get to the circus. "Maybe they can take someone else," he thought. Mark immediately called Lisa so she could make other arrangements.

"Not this time!" came Lisa's curt reply. "Jackie has been looking forward to this for weeks; you are not going to abandon her on this one.

"She is five years old and absolutely adores you," Lisa continued. "One day she will be a teenager and may not want anything to do with you if you don't build a relationship with her now. You, Mr. Sunshine, are taking us to the circus today. Be home by 3:30."

Lisa was right. Time with Jackie was precious and temporary. Hard as it was, he began adjusting his schedule to leave by mid-afternoon.

Arriving home late, Mark ran into the house and called out, "Are you ready to go yet?"

Lisa appeared from the living room, "Late again, huh?"

"Don't start with me," he replied with a roll of his eyes as Jackie ran toward him.

Dressed in red shirt, purple pants and black shoes, she said, "Daddy, how do I look?"

"Perfect," he said, giving her a hug.

Mark thought about changing into some comfortable clothes, but since they were already late, he quickly took Jackie in his arms and they all headed for the circus.

∽⟨⟨⟨⟨⟨⟩⟩⟩∽

But Where's the Top Hat?

After stepping on several feet while finding their seats in the dark, Mark, Lisa and Jackie settled in to enjoy what was left of the first half of the circus. The look on Mark's face made it obvious he didn't want to be there.

"At least *try* to act like you're enjoying yourself," Lisa whispered. "Don't ruin Jackie's day, too." He nodded agreement, but still wished he could get back to work.

It wasn't long before Mark recalled why children love the circus. One minute Jackie's eyes were fixed on the tightrope walkers, watching every move they made, the next, she was laughing at the clowns in their slapstick routines, then she stood to imitate the moves of the dancing bears as her attention moved from ring to ring.

Thoughts about work kept Mark's enthusiasm in check. He wondered what the outcome of the budget meeting was that afternoon and if Karen got the report finished and sent to the corporate office.

A tug on his arm brought him back to reality. All this excitement had led Jackie to one inevitable conclusion: "I'm hungry," she said. While he dreaded the walk back to the lobby, he saw it as an opportunity to check on things at work.

As he stepped into the hallway, Mark looked at his phone to see if anyone had called. Urgent messages. One was from his assistant about a proposal that was due next week. The deadline had slipped his mind. He called two members of his staff, but they had gone home for the day. He made a couple of quick notes on the back of his circus ticket to jog his memory later.

He was about to make another phone call when he heard the music rising, signaling that the first half was almost over. He hurried toward the food vendors to beat the intermission rush.

The aroma of hot dogs, peanuts, melted cheese and popcorn reminded him that *his* favorite part of the circus was the food. It made him want to walk up to the counter and say, "I'll take three of everything!"

A lack of willpower, in fact, was part of his challenge. He would sometimes reason that he could eat certain foods because he would "work them off" at the gym. Unfortunately, he rarely made it to the gym because he allowed other things to fill his schedule. He ordered hot dogs for Jackie and Lisa and popcorn for himself, then headed back to his seat.

Mark handed the food to the girls and sat down to listen to the rest of his messages. Jackie kept talking about all he had missed. She bounced around the seats with her pent-up energy and excitement. Mark motioned with his free hand to get her to stop so he could hear his messages.

After three unsuccessful attempts to calm her down, Mark looked at Lisa and said, "Can you please deal with her for a minute? I have to make this call." Lisa gave him a "we'll talk later" glance, then struck up a conversation with Jackie about the roustabouts setting up for the next act in one of the rings.

Mark made his phone call, but the person he needed to talk to was unavailable. He sighed in frustration and shook his head. "Of all the days to be at the circus," he thought.

The man sitting next to Mark said, "Your daughter is a bundle of energy! *She* should be in the circus."

"If you ask me," Mark said, "she's already in one...MINE!"

Jackie noticed that Mark was off the phone. "What do you like best about the circus, Daddy?" she asked.

"I don't know," he replied. "The tigers, I guess," he said, making up an answer.

Jackie frowned. "Daddy, I did not see any tigers in the circus."

Sensing the need to lighten the moment, the stranger sitting next to Mark asked Jackie, "What is *your* favorite part of the circus so far?"

"It is the dancing bears," Jackie answered happily. She imitated their movements, stepping on Mark's feet a couple of times until he asked her to stop. Lisa joined the conversation, "Jackie, let's get you to the restroom before the second half starts."

As Jackie and Lisa stepped out into the aisle, Mark asked the stranger, "What's your favorite part of the circus?"

"Well, I enjoy the bears, but I'm actually here to watch the *entire* circus," the stranger replied.

"Really?" Mark said. "Without kids?"

"Let me explain. I'm Victor, the ringmaster with another circus that tours in a different part of the country." Victor extended his hand.

"You're a ringmaster?" Mark asked as he shook his hand.

"Yes, believe it or not. I have my top hat in the car to prove it," Victor answered.

"What are you doing here?" Mark asked.

"Our circus is on a break right now, so I decided to come and watch Dominic's show. I like to see how the other circus conducts its performance."

"What are you doing up here in the cheap seats?" Mark asked. "If I were you, I'd be down front or on the floor where all the action is."

"I hang out down there every now and then, but sometimes I like to see the action from the audience's perspective," Victor explained.

"I've never met a real ringmaster," Mark said. "What a fantastic job, considering all of the experiences you have and the people you get to meet."

When Lisa and Jackie returned, Mark introduced them to Victor. As they sat down for the second half, Victor asked Mark, "So how are *you* enjoying the circus?"

"It's OK, I guess," Mark replied. "Jackie is enjoying it, and that's the main reason I'm here."

"How did you like the performer who was juggling elephants?" asked Victor, trying to keep a straight face.

Mark laughed as he said, "Even *I* know that act didn't happen."

"Well, it may not have been performed here," Victor replied, "but it seems like you are attempting it in your own circus. Maybe I should ask how you are enjoying *your* circus."

Mark glanced at him, puzzled.

"Based on what I've seen so far, I'd say you're trying to juggle elephants," Victor said.

"I hadn't thought of it in those terms before," Mark said, "but yes, that seems like a good description of what I'm doing."

The result of trying
to juggle elephants
is that no one,
including you, is
thrilled with your
performance.

"And how's that working for you?" Victor asked.

"It's OK, I guess," Mark said, wondering what Victor was getting at.

"Well, you know that juggling elephants is impossible," Victor replied. **"The result of trying to juggle elephants is that no one, including you, is thrilled with your performance."**

While Mark wanted to ignore Victor's comment, he also was intrigued.

"You're right about that," Mark said. "There is so much to get done that I just can't seem to give any one area of my life the attention it deserves. Just when I think I've made progress by getting one elephant in motion, two more drop to the ground."

"I really want to enjoy being here, but I also need to be at work," Mark explained. "If I was at work, I would be thinking about how much I missed spending time with my family at the circus.

"So on second thought, I guess you could say my attempt at juggling elephants is not going very well," Mark concluded. "I really wasn't joking a few minutes ago about my life feeling like a three-ring circus!"

"Great!" Victor replied. "Most people don't see the value in looking at their life in such a way."

"Value?" Mark laughed. "What value could there possibly be in your life being like a circus? I meant it as a negative statement, not a positive one."

Victor smiled. "Let me ask you something. When I introduced myself, you thought it would be great to be a ringmaster. Yet you see equating your life to a circus as a negative?"

Mark grinned sheepishly. "OK, I get your point. What I was trying to say was that my life feels like a three-ring circus. Unlike this circus, however, my life seems chaotic. I wish *my* circus had the organization and entertainment I see in this one."

"Really?" Victor commented. "Interesting."

The lights flashed, signaling the second half was about to begin.

"Do me a favor in the second half," Victor said. "Observe the ringmaster. Also, look beyond the action in the rings, and watch how the acts come and go. I think you will make some interesting observations."

Mark was amused yet curious about Victor's comments.

"What can I possibly learn about my life from watching a circus?" he snickered.

Three Rings to Remember

The second half began with one ring erupting in activity, then another coming alive a few minutes later. As Mark watched, he kept thinking about what Victor had said, especially his "Watch the ringmaster" comment. Mark turned his full attention to the ring.

As the ringmaster finished announcing the dancing horses act, Mark observed closely. The Ringmaster watched the first few seconds of the performance, then walked to the second ring where the clowns were finishing up their routine.

He spoke to the next group of performers and announced their arrival. Looking over his shoulder to make sure the act was ready, he called the performers into the ring.

The ringmaster
has the greatest
impact on the
success of
the circus.

Finishing his announcement, he quickly moved to the third ring where the trapeze act was ending and led the applause for their performance.

Mark soon realized it was the ringmaster who kept the three rings connected to each other and who sustained the audience's interest.

It would be so easy to miss a certain act or part of an act in a specific ring, but the ringmaster drew the audience's attention to the right ring at just the right moment so no one would miss any of the action.

Mark turned to Victor and shared his first insight. "OK, I see how the rings are connected. It's the ringmaster, isn't it? He is the link between the rings."

"Yes," Victor replied. "Now let me ask you a question. Who, then, has the biggest role in determining the success of the circus?" Victor asked.

"I guess it would be the ringmaster," Mark replied.

"Exactly," Victor said. **"The ringmaster has the greatest impact on the success of the circus."**

"When I first started with the circus, I thought certain acts were what made it successful," Victor recalled. "There *are* acts that some people like more than others, but once I became a ringmaster, I realized it was how I tied all the acts together that was important."

"That seems like a huge responsibility," Mark said.

"It is," replied Victor, "but it is also extremely rewarding. When I stand at the edge of the rings after the performance and see the people exiting with smiles, I know I have fulfilled my purpose."

The ringmaster cannot be in all three rings at once.

"Ever get caught in one ring when you should have been in another?" Mark asked.

"Sure," Victor replied. "In training, I would get so caught up with the act in one ring that I would forget to be ready to work in the next ring! I struggled to find a way to manage my time.

"It was not until Dominic got tired of seeing me moving around like I had been shot out of a cannon that he gave me the best advice I have ever received."

"What was it?" Mark asked.

"The ringmaster cannot be in all three rings at once," replied Victor.

"I have to give my full attention to the ring I am in and, when it's time, I must move to the other ring as quickly as possible."

Mark realized that he was always evaluating his life by *everything* that was going on. At any given moment, he might be thinking about work, his personal life and his relationships—and things often appeared beyond his control.

Mark turned back to the performance and began to notice that although the circus had much going on in all three rings, the way the acts in each ring came and went was anything but chaotic.

There were always roustabouts ready to take the lion cages or clown cars away. The next act for each ring was just beyond the spotlights, ready to begin at a moment's notice.

Mark thought about what his life would be like if it was as well orchestrated as the circus. In that moment, he chuckled. Victor's comments were making sense again.

Mark reflected on what he had noticed about the movement of the acts in and out of the rings. He wondered what would happen if he focused on just one area of his life like he did with the acts in one circus ring. Would he see things differently?

Mark turned to Victor. "I see your point about how the acts come and go so smoothly in one ring. How do I make that happen in my life?" he asked.

"It consists of two parts," Victor replied. "The first step is to have a plan, much like the program you have in your hand. Most acts follow each other in a well-developed order that is already known to work. The ringmaster simply follows the order.

"If you really want to make the performance effective, however, you have to review the acts before bringing them into the ring," Victor added.

"You mean at rehearsal?" Mark asked.

"No, I mean just before you bring one into the ring," Victor replied.

Sipping his soda, Victor continued. "Remember Murphy's Law? If anything can go wrong, it will? It definitely applies to the circus. A constant stream of people, animals and props have to be in position and ready to perform. It is not unusual for things to happen that prevent an act from being brought into the ring at the exact moment it is expected to appear.

"As the ringmaster, you have to know when to change the order or do something else," he continued. "If you aren't sensitive to the changes around you, you can look pretty ridiculous announcing an act that's not ready to go into the ring. **The ringmaster always reviews the next act before bringing it into the ring.**"

"How do you know when to change the order?" Mark asked.

"Simple," Victor replied. "You look to see if the next act is ready. If it is, you bring it into the ring. If there is a minor problem, you tell a joke or sing or something else to fill the time. If the act is still not ready, you move on to the next act that *is* ready.

"By the way," Victor said, "have you noticed any connections between the three rings and the areas of your life?"

"I know that work is one ring. I'm just not sure I've figured out the others," Mark replied.

Mark's thoughts were interrupted by a shrill scream. "Daddy, there are the tigers! Remember, that's your favorite part." Mark smiled at Victor, recalling his comment at intermission.

As Jackie turned her attention to the acrobats in the left ring, Mark looked at her and knew he had identified part of the second ring of his life. It was Jackie, but not just Jackie. It was Lisa, his parents and the other relationships in his life.

The ringmaster
always reviews
the next act before
bringing it into
the ring.

In circus terms, he would have to say that he didn't have many acts lined up for this ring. He made some time for Lisa, but they had not had a "date night" in several months.

His relationship with Jackie had changed much in the past year. Mark could not recall the last time he sat on the floor with her for a tea party.

He recalled times in recent memory when Jackie would say, "Watch me daddy," and he would respond "I am" without really looking at her because he was too busy with something else.

Mark also thought of some friends who had been asking him to take a day off for a round of golf or some fishing, but he wouldn't let himself take the time away from work. When he saw his friends later, they would tell of their great golf scores or who caught the biggest fish. He always told himself that he would take the next opportunity to go with them. Several "next" times had come and gone, and Mark missed the positive energy generated by spending time with his friends.

"If my work or professional life is one ring, I think I found my second ring," Mark said to Victor.

"What is it?" he asked.

"It's my relationships," Mark replied.

"Right again," Victor said. "You can imagine how ineffective this circus would be if there were only acts going on in one ring. **The key to the success of the circus is having quality acts in all three rings.**"

The key to
the success of
the circus is having
quality acts in
all three rings.

As Mark was reflecting on his new insights, the shout of "Cotton candy, get your cotton candy!" jolted him.

"May I have some, please?" Jackie asked.

"With manners like that," Mark said, "of course you can." He bought two bags, handing one to Jackie and keeping one for himself.

Staring down at the swirled strands of sugar, he shook his head as he began eating it. "This is the last thing I need," he thought.

"Of all the things I take care of in my life, taking care of myself is probably where I do the worst job."

"Aha," he thought. "That's the final ring. My 'self' ring."

Looking at this one really hurt. A few years back, when a close friend suffered a heart attack, Mark committed to living a healthier life. He had not followed through on his plan.

He thought about the past week at work when the elevators were not working and he was forced to walk up four flights of stairs to his office. Once there, he was so short of breath that he could hardly talk for the first couple of minutes.

Mark also thought of the books stacked on his nightstand. The ones he had intended to read this year but was too mentally exhausted at night to open. The days of coworkers asking him for a recommendation on a good book to read were gone.

Mark realized "self" time had become very limited. He even stopped doing little things like playing fetch with his dog when he got home from work. Those few moments had always helped him transition from the hectic pace of work and renewed his energy for the evening ahead.

Mark leaned over to Victor and said, "If I had the ringmaster's job, I wouldn't have to work out at the gym."

Victor laughed and replied, "There is no question that being the ringmaster is a busy job. At any given moment, you have to ask yourself, 'Which ring should I be in at this moment?' and then, 'Which acts should be in the ring right now?' "

Mark now knew that one of his challenges was that he was not being the ringmaster of *his* own circus. He was just jumping from ring to ring, accepting whatever acts were easiest and most convenient to have in a ring at that moment.

He realized that while things were seemingly going well in his professional ring, there was nothing going on in his self ring. Eventually, that hurt his performance in his professional ring, because he wasn't taking care of the other areas of his life. As the ringmaster of his circus, he should have recognized the problem and made some adjustments.

Mark's analysis would have continued if not for the rising music that signaled the grand finale. The performers marched around the perimeter of the rings, offering a final goodbye to the audience.

Jackie, although exhausted from the day's events, waved to them and said to Mark, "Oh, Daddy, thank you for bringing me to the circus!"

Victor leaned over to Mark and said, "Aren't you glad you moved into your relationship ring today?"

"Yes," Mark said. "With what I have going on at work, I know I won't be able to have this kind of time with her for quite a while."

As Jackie pulled on his sleeve to be carried, Mark reached out to shake Victor's hand.

"Victor, it's been a good evening for *all* of us. When you told me that it would be a positive thing for my life to be like a circus, I thought you were crazy.

"You really know your way around the circus, though," Mark continued, "and you made some powerful points. In fact, you have me thinking of even more questions about how the circus applies to my life."

"Well, Dominic has been a pretty good teacher," Victor replied. "Who knows what else I will learn from him this week."

"You're going to be here all week?" Mark asked.

"Yes. Our circus is on a two-week break," Victor explained. "We ought to meet here sometime this week. I'll introduce you to Dominic. He can tackle most any question you have."

"I'd really enjoy that," Mark replied, "But I don't know how I can fit it into my schedule."

"I understand," Victor replied.

After thinking about it for a second, Mark changed his mind and said, "I might be able to break away at lunch on Friday. Would that work for you?"

"I think so," said Victor. "Noon is fine; the peanuts and hot dogs are on me."

They shook hands, and Mark continued toward the exit.

Programs, Get Your Programs!

At breakfast the next morning, Jackie giggled as Mark hummed a tune from the previous night's circus.

"Boy, I think both of you kids enjoyed the circus," Lisa said.

Mark and Jackie looked at each other with coy smiles and continued eating.

Finishing his last drop of orange juice, Mark stood up, kissed Lisa and Jackie and said, "I'm off to the next act in *my* circus," which left both of them confused. Mark, however, knew exactly what he was saying.

Once at work, Mark had his assistant clear his schedule for the next hour. He closed his door, sat at his desk and took out three pieces of paper. On each one he drew a ring, labeling one "professional," one "self" and one "relationships."

"Today," he mused, "is the day I start becoming the ringmaster of *my* circus."

As Mark began looking at his three rings, he tried to recall some of the things Victor had said. He jotted a few thoughts down on one of the papers:

☞ *The ringmaster cannot be in all three rings at once.*

☞ *The ringmaster always reviews the next act before bringing it into the ring.*

☞ *The key to the success of the circus is having quality acts in all three rings.*

☞ *Which ring should I be in at this moment?*

☞ *What acts should I be focusing on right now?*

With those thoughts in mind, Mark placed the papers marked "relationships" and "self" behind the one marked "professional," because there was no question which ring he should be focusing on at the moment. He then listed his current work-related projects and activities.

Mark remembered the roustabouts working hard between acts to change the stage or props, and he began listing the necessary resources or people he needed to successfully complete each of his "acts."

He suddenly felt overwhelmed. "I couldn't get all of these things done this week if I had 36 hours in a day," he thought.

Then he remembered Victor's question: Which acts should be in the ring right now?

Mark knew that he would need to order—or line up—his acts to ensure the most important items got completed first. He reviewed his list again and began numbering the items according to their importance.

He was just about to begin his first task of updating a company policy when he remembered something else Victor had said about reviewing an act before bringing it into the ring.

Mark recognized that while the task of updating a policy was important, there was information he needed from the human resources department that would not be available until next week. Working on that task now would not be wise because he could not complete it in an efficient manner.

He made a note to himself and added it to his lineup for next week, when the missing information would be available.

The sense of direction Mark felt as he worked through the morning was both exciting and liberating. Although he was interrupted several times by coworkers and unexpected events, having a plan helped him get quickly back on track.

He even found himself adding other acts to the lineup. He knew he would not get to them this week, but at least they would be ready the next time he planned his program.

At lunch that day, Mark purchased a sandwich from the company cafeteria and settled back into his office. He laid out the paper with the ring marked relationships and mentally reviewed the process he had used for his professional ring:

☞ *List the acts that should be in the ring.*

☞ *Review the program (list of acts).*

☞ *Look for new acts that may need to be brought into the lineup.*

☞ *Line up the acts.*

☞ *Determine how to make the existing acts successful.*

While most acts listed in his professional ring focused on tasks or meetings, Mark found himself listing people in his relationship ring. He listed Jackie, Lisa, his parents and Joe, a friend he had been meaning to call.

Looking back over the notes from his conversation with Victor, he saw "Success is having quality acts in all three rings." Mark thought about other people he should bring into his relationship ring.

It was quite clear that he needed to get in touch with his friends to schedule a golf outing. He knew it would be good to catch up with those guys. After adding a couple more names, Mark began to line up his acts.

He started with Jackie, because he already knew what he needed to do with her. He would get some poster paper on the way home from work and help her draw a picture of something from the circus.

He made a note to call Dean and set up a time to have lunch together. Mark also made some other notes, including scheduling a time to have the new neighbors over for dinner and to call his friend John who he had not seen at church the past two Sundays.

Mark liked the clarity of direction he got from the exercise. He leaned back in his chair for a stretch before moving back into his professional ring.

Appearing in This Ring...

I s something wrong with your car?" one neighbor asked.

Another shouted, "Do you need a ride?"

Mark had to smile. It had been a long time since he had walked around the block his home was on, and the comments from his neighbors affirmed this.

Before going to bed the previous evening, Mark had taken out the third piece of paper marked self and looked more closely at the acts listed there.

Aware that very little was happening in that part of his life, Mark committed to doing *something*. Although he knew he needed to do more than walk a few blocks, at least he was bringing some type of act into this ring.

Another important act in his self ring would take place at lunch.

On Wednesdays, Mark and several other managers went to a local restaurant for the pizza buffet. It was so good! Mark knew, however, that if he was ever going to lose his extra thirty pounds, he had to start today, not tomorrow or next week.

Mark chose to order a salad instead of hitting the buffet—the ribbing from his friends was annoying but expected. He simply laughed with them.

After arriving home from work, Mark had the usual routine of picking Jackie up from dance class, checking on his parents and discussing the day's activities with Lisa.

These once seemingly trivial events now took on a more significant meaning. Mark knew they were part of his relationship ring—part of what made his life successful by his standards.

Jackie's drawing from the previous evening confirmed his insight. Instead of just drawing an act or two from the circus, Jackie added the audience, including herself, Mark and Lisa grinning from ear to ear.

Mark also changed his bedtime routine. Rather than channel surf until he found something to occupy his mind, he picked up a book from his nightstand, dusted off the cover and read for twenty minutes before turning out the light.

Mark had planned to look at his self ring again on Thursday evening, but things were hectic at work. Two staff members had a disagreement over who was responsible for a mistake, and Mark was getting pressure from his boss about not meeting a deadline.

Challenges at work threw him off his schedule for the rest of the day. He realized that he should not have created a lineup that had so many acts in his professional ring. He didn't leave any room for interruptions.

Mark went directly to his monthly civic organization meeting after work. Arriving home late, he stopped in Jackie's room, hoping to catch her before she fell asleep. He gave her a kiss and adjusted her covers. Jackie mumbled something and fell fast asleep again.

As he stepped into the bedroom, he was annoyed to find a pile of clean, unfolded clothes on his side of the bed. "What's up with this?" he thought.

He wanted to shove the pile over to Lisa's side of the bed and let her deal with it. "After the day I've had, the least she could do is take care of the laundry," he mumbled.

"I heard that," came a response from behind. Lisa had just walked into the room.

"Ever think about how hectic *my* day might have been?" she snapped. "You don't have a monopoly on a busy life, you know."

She and Mark spent the next few minutes griping to each other about why things were not getting done around the house.

Mark was a word away from making a stinging comment when he remembered his earlier thought about working on his relationships. From past events, he knew that if he made the negative comment, it would only make the situation worse.

He looked at Lisa and simply responded, "I'm sorry. I shouldn't have gotten so worked up about it. I know you have been busy getting things in order at school."

"It's OK, Mark," Lisa replied. "We both have been too busy lately. It just seems like we are running in opposite directions all the time. I'm sorry, too."

"Feel like you're trying to juggle elephants?" Mark asked.

"That's a good way to describe it," agreed Lisa.

Recognizing a chance to work on his relationship ring, Mark asked, "How about we fold these clothes and talk?"

Lisa was shocked, but the chance to get the clothes put away faster got her attention.

"Sure," she said. As they worked, they discussed ways to help each other with their busy schedules. They committed to a weekly planning session to coordinate the family's activities. With the clothes and their schedules in better order, they turned in for the evening.

The Heart of the Circus

I just don't want to work here anymore! I found something better. Here's my notice." Mark could not believe Jay's comment. He had hired Jay two years ago and thought Jay would be with the company for a long time.

He had, in fact, become a key member of Mark's team. Jay's responsibilities matched with his interests well, and his compensation package was one of the best in the company for someone in his position.

Mark admired the way Jay was fully engaged in his work. He had noticed a slight decrease in Jay's determination lately, but reasoned that it was probably something minor. Mark wondered why he would just leave.

In the ensuing conversation, the only thing Mark could get out of Jay was that the working relationship he had with several members of the staff had become less than ideal.

Jay saw one as too demanding, while another individual always expected him to "clean up the mess" left by another employee's carelessness.

These situations apparently had drained Jay of much of his creative energy, and he was frustrated that he could not give more attention to his own responsibilities.

Following that difficult discussion, Mark welcomed the opportunity to get away from the office for awhile. Being around the staff sometimes drained him, and losing Jay meant he would have to start the complex hiring process. He could already feel the uneasiness in his stomach.

Driving to the circus arena, Mark smiled as he thought about using some strategies from the animal trainer to get his staff back in line. Although frustrated, he had to admit that the circus concepts were helpful.

It was now almost automatic for Mark to ask himself, "Which ring should I be in right now?" It helped him focus more in the moment, whether at work or at home, especially when he added the second question, "What act should I be focusing on?"

His challenge, however, was that his rings were too crowded. He could get to the correct ring without much trouble, but lining up the right acts was still difficult.

Since there was no afternoon circus performance, Mark was able to drive through the main gate and ask the security guard where to park. He grabbed his bag and made his way to the main entrance. Victor was waiting for him.

"Acts in your professional ring go overtime today?" Victor asked.

"Not only that," Mark replied, "but I lost one of my best performers today because he couldn't get along with some other people in the circus."

"Sorry to hear that," Victor said as they shook hands.

"Still think the circus can teach you something about life?" Victor asked.

"Judge for yourself," Mark said as he pulled out one of his ring sheets.

"Quite impressive," Victor responded as he looked over the pages. "Looks like you're getting the picture."

"I am," replied Mark.

"What are all of these items that are marked out and then written down again?" Victor asked.

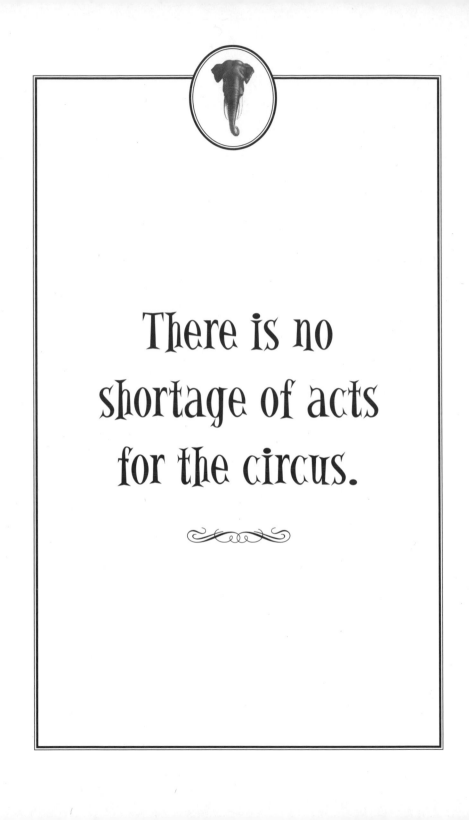

There is no shortage of acts for the circus.

"I'm still struggling with how to plan the lineup of my acts," Mark explained. "It's helpful when I ask myself simple questions such as 'Which ring should I be in right now?' and 'What acts should I be focusing on?'

"My work life—or professional ring—seems more productive, and I feel more engaged in many of my tasks.

"Acknowledging the presence of a self ring has been good," he continued, "and I'm doing better in my relationship ring.

"The simple answer to your question is I struggle because I have so much going on in all areas of my life at one time," Mark explained. "Add my staff to the lineup, and I almost feel like the circus is running me instead of me running the circus."

"Well put, Mark," Victor replied. **"There is no shortage of acts for the circus.** Before you leave today, I want you to talk with Dominic. I had the same discussion with him when I first started as a ringmaster."

Mark and Victor walked into the arena.

"There he is," Victor said, pointing to a tall, dark-haired man standing in the midst of a small group of people. "We'll catch up with him later."

They bought lunch from a vending cart and walked back to the arena.

"Victor, I understand that I have three rings in my life, and I recognize the need to focus on a specific ring. My frustration comes in deciding *which* acts should be in my rings. I'm not sure I'm actually headed toward the performance of a lifetime, you might say."

"To deal with that issue, let's go to the floor and get into the rings," Victor said.

They walked down the steps, across the sawdust and into the center ring.

"Look up into the arena," Victor said. "Imagine that it's a typical night at the circus. What would you see?"

"People in the seats," Mark answered.

"Good," Victor said. "And what do all these people have in common?"

"They like peanuts?" Mark joked.

"Very funny," Victor said. "Seriously, what do they all have in common?"

"They want to see a good performance," Mark replied.

"Exactly! And if they don't?" Victor asked.

"They won't come back to see the circus again," Mark surmised.

"How do you think that impacts the way we look at the acts we put in the circus?" Victor asked.

"You have to choose the best ones," Mark replied.

"Correct," Victor responded.

"My performance director and I have no shortage of acts that we could place in the lineup. Not a day goes by that we couldn't add new acts to the circus.

"One reason we don't add them, however, is because they would not contribute to the overall success of the circus.

"The circus exists to entertain audiences of all ages and to be a profitable organization that can continue to operate for years," Victor explained. "To accomplish those goals, we must have quality acts in each ring. It all begins with recognizing that **every act must serve a purpose**."

Victor continued, "Choosing acts based on your purpose works best when it becomes a habit. It's easy to make a wrong choice based solely on emotion, convenience or pressure from others who don't have a good understanding of your purpose.

"Make the wrong choice, and you will sometimes bring a bad act into your circus," Victor chuckled. "Then you have the 'dancing lizards' dilemma."

"I can't wait to hear this one," Mark replied with a laugh.

"It was about seven years ago," Victor began, "My first year as a ringmaster. Just after the season started, one of the clowns came to me and wanted to add another act.

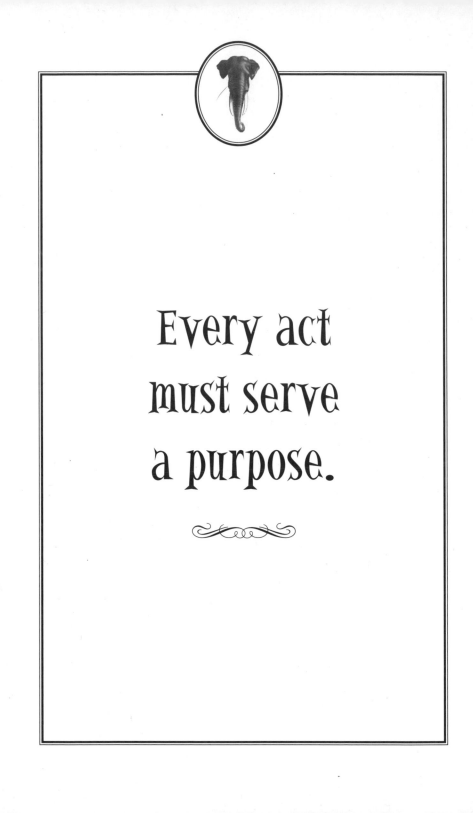

Every act must serve a purpose.

"Normally, no new acts are allowed without reviewing them first," he continued. "He promised that this new act would be nothing like I had ever seen. I was busy, so I gave in and waited to see his big surprise.

"When it came time for the clowns to demonstrate their individual gags, this clown opened a box. He sat three lizards on a table, signaled for the music to start, and the lizards moved their heads, seemingly to the beat of the music," Victor recalled with a grin.

"The audience had no idea what he was trying to do. I was embarrassed for both of us," Victor said. "After the performance, I told him I never wanted to see the dancing lizards routine again."

Mark reflected on Victor's comments and realized that he had put some bad acts in his circus over the past year.

"I can see where I have made some incorrect choices in my lineup," Mark said, "but my greatest anxiety doesn't come from choosing between a bad act and a good one, but choosing between two or three good ones."

"We have the same challenge in the circus," Victor replied. "That's when I have to remind myself that **not all acts belong in my circus**. We cannot be all things to all people. Choices have to be made."

"But that's what I'm saying," Mark answered. "How do I choose *which* acts to bring into my ring?"

"As I said earlier, it starts with asking yourself whether it fulfills your purpose for that ring," Victor replied. "With purpose in mind, the next question is, 'Do I have the resources to make the act successful?'

"I review some fantastic acts, but we have no room for them in the lineup right now," Victor said.

"Couldn't you just drop one of the existing acts?" Mark asked.

"Sure, that's possible, and we do," Victor responded. "But realize that decision could have a negative impact on the overall circus. Remember, if we plan our acts correctly, every act serves a purpose."

Victor's words took Mark back to a situation his company experienced a couple of years ago.

A new product was launched at a time when the marketing department was already working at a breakneck pace. Research was not properly done, the marketing plan was ineffectual, and the go-to-market strategy was weak.

The product failed to have an impact in the marketplace because time and resources were just not available to successfully launch it. The product was good, but the timing was bad.

Victor continued, "I also see acts that would be perfect for our circus, but we don't have the physical space for them on our traveling train.

"Last year, we auditioned someone who gets shot out of a cannon. It was the best act like that I have seen in years. The problem was that when we looked at the space he would need to transport that big cannon, we had to say no."

"Do you ever get another chance to bring those acts into the circus?" Mark asked.

"Sometimes," said Victor. "We added one act five years after the first time we reviewed it. We are constantly looking at ways to improve our circus, but sometimes the resources are just not there.

"Circumstances change, performers retire or leave. The circus may introduce a new theme for the year. Any number of things can change our mind about an act and cause us to use it as long as it fits with our purpose.

"We also believe that only quality acts belong in a circus," Victor added. "Even though it may not be right for our circus, it's a shame for the act not to find a home. We may refer them to Dominic to see if his circus could use them, or we put them in touch with another circus. There are always circuses looking for new and better acts.

"Another part of our strategy involves looking not at individual acts, but at the overall order of those acts in the lineup.

"Line up the acts based on what will create an effective performance. In the end, they may not remember a specific act, but they *will* remember how they felt at the circus."

"Your process obviously works well for this circus," Mark said. "Can we stop for a moment so I can make some notes?"

"Before you write anything, one last consideration needs to be made," Victor said. "It's a lesson I learned the hard way. In fact, I try to forget the experience, as often as possible, that led to this valuable lesson."

"Let's hear it," Mark replied with a chuckle.

Victor began, "Not long after I began training to be a ringmaster, I started questioning how Dominic had the acts arranged in the circus. I thought we needed to liven things up a little and pick up the pace. Dominic finally let me have my wish one night.

"About a week prior to the performance, Dominic told me to arrange the acts in each ring as I saw best."

"How did it go?" Mark asked.

"It was horrible!" Victor said, with his head in his hands.

"At first, the upbeat pace seemed to be working well. Then came a point where I had scheduled several major acts at the same time. The roustabouts were scrambling to keep everything in place, and the audience got confused because there was so much going on.

"The second half wasn't much better," he continued. "Because I scheduled major acts together, the audience lost interest when there was a lull in the action.

"We made it through the night, but Dominic promised the staff that he would not let me arrange the schedule again until I had learned more.

"And I would never *want* to do it again, either," Victor added. "It seemed like a good idea at the time. It nearly killed me, trying to keep up with the acts and trying to be in all three rings at once. I was physically, mentally and emotionally exhausted."

"How does that experience apply to me?" Mark asked.

"Look at a successful three-ring circus performance," Victor answered. **"The circus maintains its effectiveness and efficiency by scheduling major acts at different times.**

"It would be almost impossible to have enough staff to have all of the major acts take place at the same time, or even to have them follow each other," Victor explained. "Scheduling the acts at different times enables them to be managed better, and the ringmaster can function at his best, as well."

"OK, Victor," Mark said, "while you recover from recalling your traumatic experience, can I write some of these things down?"

"Sure. Just don't use me as your example of creating a bad performance," Victor joked.

Mark sat down and recorded the key points of their conversation:

☞ *Not all acts belong in my circus.*

☞ *Does it fulfill my purpose?*

☞ *Do I have the resources to make it successful?*

☞ *Line up my acts based on what will create an effective performance.*

☞ *Maintain my efficiency and effectiveness by scheduling major acts at different times.*

The Performers

As Mark reflected on his notes, he wished his staff could hear Victor's words about lining up the right acts. He thought back to last week. A member of his staff failed to get an important report to his boss, even after Mark had reminded him several times. When Mark got called into the boss' office, he knew it was not for a positive reason.

Mark was frustrated because he didn't think he should have to constantly remind someone of something that was already part of his job responsibilities.

"Victor," Mark said, "I'm beginning to realize how much other people can affect my circus. Sometimes my staff doesn't seem to listen to me; I feel like we're communicating on different levels.

"If you could help me solve my employee problems, that would *really* make my circus more memorable," Mark quipped.

The relationship
between the
ringmaster and the
performers affects
the success of
the circus.

"Take this morning, for instance, I had no clue that one of my employees was so unhappy with his job. To make matters worse, I have new information from him that other troubles may be brewing in my department. If I can't keep my staff engaged in their tasks, how am I supposed to stay focused?"

"I have some ideas, but the expert in this area is Dominic," Victor said. "He was one of my mentors in how to lead others. He always says that **the relationship between the ringmaster and the performers affects the success of the circus.**"

Victor noticed that Dominic was no longer busy, so he motioned for him to join their conversation.

"Well, well, is this the new recruit to clean up after the elephants?" Dominic asked in his booming announcer voice.

Victor smiled. "Afraid not, Dominic. This is Mark. He was at the circus on Monday night, and we began that talk you had with me a few years ago."

"I see," Dominic replied. "And are you still trying to juggle elephants?" he asked Mark.

"Not so much in acts where I'm the only performer," Mark replied. "But trying to lead my staff makes me feel like I am."

"You mean they just don't seem like willing performers in your circus?" Dominic asked insightfully.

"I couldn't have said it better," Mark replied.

"I think I can help with your juggling dilemma, but first we better get out of the way.

"Duck!!" he yelled. At that moment, a member of the trapeze team sailed overhead.

"It's rehearsal time. Let's move to the seats." They walked to some seats near the center ring.

"Before we get into specifics, Mark, let me tell you a little about my background," Dominic began. "I started out many years ago as a roustabout. It was hard work, but I stuck with it.

"From there, I became an assistant with the animal trainer. I was even a clown for a time. In fact, I think I have spent some time in almost every job the circus has to offer, even cleaning up after the elephants.

"As a result, I have learned that it takes every person doing the right job at the right moment to make the circus successful."

"Go on," Mark said.

"It all begins with the ringmaster," Dominic explained. "The ringmaster must be totally focused on his role. He needs to be intimately familiar with the lineup, know the performers, and be able to keep the circus moving at the proper pace. The performers look to the ringmaster for leadership and direction. The ringmaster has the greatest influence on the success of the circus."

"Seems like I have heard that somewhere before," Mark said, glancing at Victor.

As Dominic looked out at the rehearsing performers, he said, "What I have found in my years with the circus is that every act holds a lesson in how to work with people more effectively.

"Take this trapeze act, for instance. Many years ago, I filled in for one of the performers while they recovered from the flu. I just held the bar, but I gained many new insights about teamwork.

"I learned that every member of the act is important. If just one person doesn't carry out their responsibility, the whole team suffers.

"Look at the person on that platform. Do you know what his job is?"

"No," Mark replied.

"His job is to pass the bar to a member of his team as they swing from the other side," Dominic said.

"That doesn't seem so difficult," Mark replied.

"Oh really?" Dominic commented. "What if that person said, 'I'm not the star; no one notices me in the dark.' Based on their lack of enthusiasm, they get sloppy and swing the bar at the wrong time, and the performer misses it. What would happen?"

Mark realized how he had underestimated the person's value. "The performer would fall," he said.

"Exactly," Dominic replied with a nod.

"Remember that **every team member is important and has to be fully engaged to make the act successful**. That's true whether the "team" is a department, organization or family."

Every team member is important and has to be fully engaged to make the act successful.

They turned their attention to the commotion in the left ring, where the animal trainer was working with one of his assistants on getting a tiger to jump from one platform to another.

"John is so patient with his animals. Good thing he's just as patient with his assistant," Dominic observed.

"What do you mean?" asked Mark.

"Well, his assistant thinks being an animal trainer is all about showing the animals who's boss," explained Dominic.

"Cracking the whip, so to speak, is necessary, because if someone doesn't establish expectations and remind the animals of the consequences of misbehavior, the act would be unsafe and ultimately a failure.

"Mark, please understand that I am not saying people are animals, but over the years I have seen many performers come and go. With each new performer or group, we clearly explain expectations and the consequences of failing to meet those expectations. I guess you could call that cracking the whip.

"Some performers rise to those expectations immediately," Dominic said. "Others need reminders about the expectations, and still others seem to be oblivious to everything we tell them.

"It would be easy to just dismiss all those who don't comply immediately with expectations we set for them. Just like it would be easy to get rid of a tiger that doesn't learn to perform on command as quickly as the others.

Constantly offer
positive reinforcement
for good behavior,
and consistently give
constructive feedback
for negative behavior.

"However, an effective animal trainer recognizes that discipline is a small part of the training process. Getting to know the animal is much more important. Once he understands the animal, he can work *with* the animal's personality instead of always trying to force the desired behavior.

"It's the same with people. Once you get to know an individual, you can better understand how to fully engage their energies to accomplish a specific goal or task."

Mark thought immediately of Jay. He recalled his initial interview with him, in which Jay had spelled out so clearly what motivated him. Mark had been too busy to recognize that Jay was not being challenged in a way that was motivating to him. Mark realized that his failure to notice the warning signs was now costing him one of his most promising employees.

Dominic continued. "Watching the animal trainer also showed me the need to **constantly offer positive reinforcement for good behavior, and consistently give constructive feedback for negative behavior**. A lack of reinforcement or feedback can create a lack of desire to succeed or even to meet basic expectations."

Mark thought about a manager he had in a previous company who never appeared unless something was wrong. His lack of praise for Mark's work was a key reason he left the company. He just did not feel appreciated.

"What have we here?" called a voice. "A couple of people trying to watch the circus for free?"

Dominic laughed. "Yeah, and the show's not bad if they just had a better ringmaster."

"Mark, this is April, our general manager."

"Pleased to meet you, Mark," she said. "I apologize for interrupting your meeting, but I wanted to let you know, Dominic, that Sergei just found out his mother is very sick. I have arranged his travel home and thought I would send flowers on behalf of all of us. I just wanted you to know."

"Of course," Dominic said. "Thanks for your attention to detail."

"No problem," April replied. "That's my job. Now if you will excuse me, I need to check on a few other members of our group. Have fun at the circus, Mark."

April jogged up the steps, and the threesome turned their attention back to the circus.

"And I guess you had that job at one time too?" Mark said jokingly.

"Not in a large circus like this one," Dominic replied, "but I have had that responsibility."

"But her job doesn't seem to be about the circus," Mark said.

"April may not seem like an act in terms of a trapeze troupe or animal trainer, but her role is vital to our success as a circus.

"You see, we have high expectations of our people. They work long hours, travel extensively and rarely get a break. Some travel with their families; others are here alone.

"People could feel pretty insignificant in this crazy environment. It's April's job to make sure they have what they need to be happy, productive members of the team."

"So April's job is to help fix their problems?"

"It goes far beyond that," Dominic replied. "See that clown with green hair? That's Bruce. A few weeks ago, he was working in a concession stand. Staff members began complaining about his poor attitude. He was rude to customers and just didn't seem to care.

"The staff almost had everyone convinced that management needed to get rid of him. The concessions manager alerted April to the situation and said, 'See if you can find out what's going on with him.' "

"April put the pieces together and discovered that Bruce was bored working in concessions. April arranged an audition with the clown troupe, and now look at him. The audience loves him! He's back to being his best again.

"Just think, we nearly lost a great member of our staff because we didn't pay attention to his real needs. The work of the general manager helped me understand that **people have needs that extend way beyond the obvious ones**. April is an indispensable member of this organization."

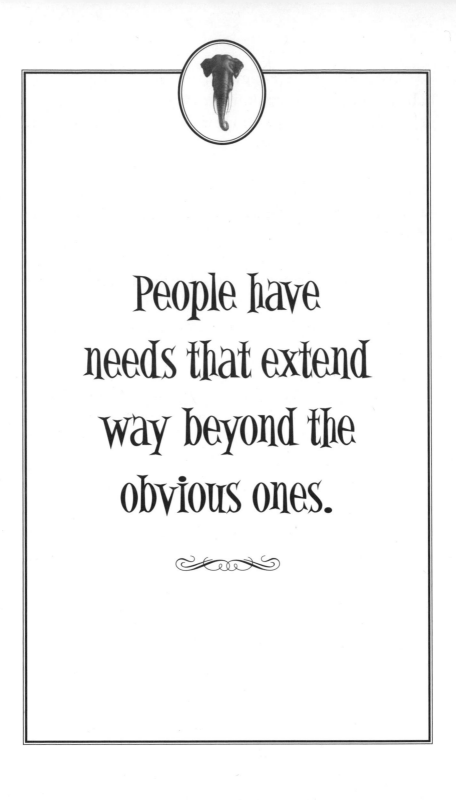

People have needs that extend way beyond the obvious ones.

"Wow," Mark exclaimed, "I wish my company had the money to hire someone for that type of position. We could call them our 'Chief Morale Officer.'"

Dominic chuckled and said, "Yes, that would be an effective title, but don't think that meeting the needs of others should be the job of just one person or limited to a formal position. *All* of us have the opportunity to focus on the needs of others whether it's a colleague, family member or neighbor. Whether we do or not depends on how much we value their contribution."

Mark looked at Dominic and said, "Speaking of clowns, I'm wondering if your next suggestion will be that I put on the red nose and pull some ridiculous stunts."

"I don't suggest that you do the pie-in-the-face routine, but think about what clowns do for the circus," Dominic replied. "They make people laugh and distract them from circumstances around them."

Victor jumped in, "I'll give you an example from Monday night. Do you remember what your daughter was doing when the bears were in the ring dancing?"

"Yes, she was standing up and dancing like them," Mark said.

"And what were you doing?" Victor asked.

"I was watching her," Mark replied.

"What if, just for a moment, you had stood up and danced with her?" Victor asked.

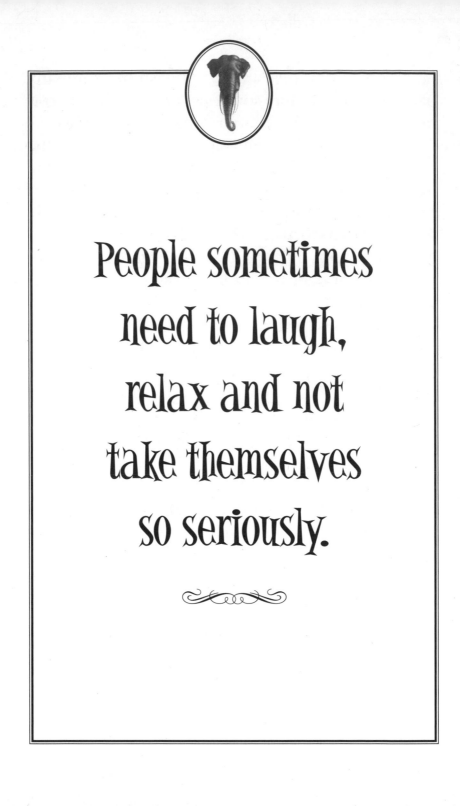

People sometimes
need to laugh,
relax and not
take themselves
so seriously.

"My wife never would have spoken to me again," Mark said with a laugh. "No, seriously, Jackie would have loved it."

"Exactly," came Victor's reply. "Being a clown isn't necessarily about elaborate performances or gags. Clowns teach us that **people sometimes need to laugh, relax and not take themselves so seriously.**"

Mark thought back to a particularly stressful time at work a few months ago. In the midst of an intense project, a department manager stopped by and asked about playing basketball.

When Mark told him he didn't have a change of clothes, the manager pulled three foam basketballs from his gym bag and placed a hoop from the bag on the door. After five minutes of slam dunks and three pointers, Mark was ready to go back to work. It was a simple mental boost during a tough time.

"Speaking of acts, I've got one scheduled in my professional ring in an hour," Mark said. "I better go complete my review before it starts."

Mark stood up, shook Dominic's hand and said, "You have been an enormous help, Dominic."

"There's much more we could talk about, Mark, but I have a hunch you'll pick it up on your own," Dominic said. "Who knows, maybe you'll get the chance to help someone else stop trying to juggle elephants."

"I'll walk out with you," Victor chimed in.

"Victor, I really appreciate your time and insight," Mark said as they approached the gate. "I never dreamed I could learn so much from something as simple as a circus. Here's my business card; please let me know if there is ever anything I can do for you."

Victor smiled. "Thanks. Maybe our circuses will cross again in the future."

They shook hands, and Mark headed for his car.

Dress Rehearsal

Several months passed, but the impact of Victor and Dominic's words and his own experience were permanently etched in Mark's mind and in his behaviors. He now always asked two questions before putting an act into one of his rings:

Does this act belong in my circus?

When should this act appear?

Mark had begun regular performances in his self ring, exercising three to four times a week. He had started running again, preparing for a 5k run that would take place in a few months. He had lost weight and seemed to have more energy for his work and his personal tasks.

Reading became part of his regular routine. In reviewing his "program" each day, he saw that he sometimes had twenty to thirty minutes of free time after lunch, and he filled the time reading a book or the newspaper before jumping back into his work. He found himself much more focused for his afternoon tasks, both mentally and physically.

Sitting on the porch one evening enjoying their planning time, Lisa asked, "What's this I hear about a daddy-daughter date?"

Mark smiled and said, "I see Jackie is no good at keeping a secret."

"Well, I would give her a pass this time," Lisa replied. "She was so excited about it, she was about to explode."

"With my new project at work, I am going to have to spend extra hours at the office," Mark said. "I will miss a few nights of bedtime stories and evening dance practices so I wanted to give Jackie and me something to look forward to over the next couple of weeks. It will help me stay focused at work, too."

"Sounds great, Mr. Popularity," Lisa said, "but what am I supposed to do while you two are gone?"

"Let me see," Mark said. "If I remember correctly, a certain someone said it would be great to have an evening at home alone. Maybe you can use the time to be in your self ring."

"I would like the time to just relax," Lisa confided, "but what is this about a 'self ring?' "

"Well, if you don't line up the right acts for your self ring, your whole circus may suffer," Mark replied with a smirk.

Lisa looked at him like he was from another planet.

"What are you talking about?" she quipped.

Mark went into the house, retrieved his papers with the three circles for the current week and returned to the porch.

He laid the papers on the table and began to explain the concept of the three rings and the other insights he had gained from Dominic, Victor and his experience at the circus.

"What I have been trying to do over the past few months," Mark said, "is take time each week to look at what should be happening in each ring of my life and then line up the acts needed to, well, create a better performance. Call me nuts, but it's working."

Lisa sat silent for a few moments, taking in what Mark said.

"I don't think you're nuts," she said. "My immediate thought was about something that happened last Thursday. I was at school and my planning period had just begun. I had papers to grade, a class project to outline and several other things I wanted to get done.

"Instead of working on them, I thought I would take a minute and call our travel agent Tom to request information about the cruise we're planning for next summer.

"When I called, Tom obviously wasn't busy, so he started outlining our options. It was exciting, and I enjoyed hearing the possibilities.

"Before I realized it, my planning time was over, and I hadn't gotten anything done.

"One thing led to another. I wasn't ready for my next class so things didn't go very smoothly. I also found myself distracted because I was frustrated with myself.

"When we had our grade level meeting after school, I wasn't as prepared as I should have been. And at home that night, I had to stay up late to finish grading papers, which cut into our time to talk.

"To top it all off, I didn't get my regular night's sleep, which made me a little cranky the next day."

"A little?" Mark said with a laugh.

"Careful," Lisa replied, smiling. "Using the idea you just talked about, I could have stopped myself before making the call and said, 'Which ring should I be in right now?'

"Then I could have focused more effectively on getting the right acts, as you call them, done," Lisa continued. "By doing so, I would have had a much more productive day and enjoyable evening.

"Talking about this has helped me realize how much I have neglected my self ring, too. Just look at that flower bed. Five years ago, I would have been out there weeding and planting. I love watching things grow.

"I think that while you and Jackie are, as you say, 'working on your relationship ring,' I'll jump into my self ring and work on those flower beds."

Preparing to retire for the evening, Lisa said to Mark, "I really like the simple concept of choosing which ring to be in and working in that ring."

"I do, too," Mark said wistfully. Lisa sensed there was something more to his comment.

"But what?" she asked.

"Well, Victor said something that I still don't quite understand. He said that major acts should be scheduled at different times in the circus. He said it was about making sure you didn't spread yourself too thin. I still don't fully get what he was trying to say."

"I think I do," Lisa said. "Think back about four years ago. Jackie was one, we decided to remodel the house, and you had taken on a new assignment at work. You were not a happy camper."

"I'll say," Mark replied. "I remember being at work trying to concentrate, but it was hard because I had been up so late working on the house. Time with Jackie was also pretty limited."

"If you were in that situation again, what do you think you would do differently?" Lisa asked.

"That's easy," Mark said. "I would put off the remodeling project for a few months."

"There's your application," Lisa said. "I remember seeing you so mentally, emotionally and physically drained all the time. If we had put off remodeling until things were less hectic, it would have helped you be more effective in your professional ring *and* in your relationship ring.

"Now, if you will excuse me, I need to bring the act called 'A Good Night's Sleep' into my self ring."

Mark laughed as they walked into the house together.

Crowded Lineup

With the new project underway, Mark needed his newfound wisdom like never before. The project was more complex than he initially thought. Even with prior planning, Mark could see that his staff was losing ground, and they were in jeopardy of not meeting the deadline.

At the next staff meeting, Mark shared his concern about their lack of productivity. He asked each staff member to give an update on their work for the benefit of everyone on the team. As the individuals shared their updates on the project, Mark wrote them on a whiteboard.

He asked, "As you look at the board, do you see any areas you could work on together to help each other?" As group members offered their thoughts, Mark wrote the additional comments on the board.

"Now I want you to set a time to meet with the people you will be working with on your tasks, so we can speed up the completion of this project."

The first few days produced no measurable results. Mark was beginning to think he had chosen the wrong way to handle the situation. A week later, however, Ben walked into his office and handed him a part of the project that was not due for another five days.

"Wow!" Mark responded. "How did this happen?"

Ben smiled and said, "I have to tell you that when you asked us to work together, I was against it. But when Chris and I started working together, I realized he had a perspective and insights that I was missing. With a little trial and error, we were able to get this done ahead of schedule. We've even begun to plan some ways we can work together on the next project."

Mark smiled as he thought about how Dominic would be proud of his efforts to pull his team together, just like the trapeze team.

A few days later, Mark was at his desk when his phone rang. It was Dan, chairman of a local civic club. Although a member of the club for many years, Mark had rarely participated in the meetings, attending only three or four a year and helping out with the annual barbecue.

After his talk with Victor about purpose in each ring, however, Mark had determined that a purpose for his self ring was to have a positive influence on his community.

He began attending meetings regularly and took a leadership role in one of their community service projects. He loved the challenge of helping people understand the need to be active in making their communities a better place to live and work.

Mark and Dan talked and joked about current events during their phone conversation, then Dan said, "You know, Mark, several of us have been talking, and we think you would be a great candidate for president of the club next year."

Mark was humbled and had an urge to say yes, but then recalled what Victor said about there being no room for another act in the circus.

"Dan, I'm flattered, but I must turn you down," he said. "I have too many things going on right now, and I would not be as focused on the position as I would need to be if I was elected.

"Lisa is just getting established in a new job, Jackie is starting school, and I've had a recent change here at work.

"I'll tell you what," he continued, "put me down as a candidate for the following year, and I'll plan ahead to fit it into my lineup."

"Lineup?" Dan asked.

Mark took a few moments to explain the concept of the three rings.

"So you see, Dan, while I really would like to add serving as president as an act in one of my rings, my lineup is just too full right now."

Although disappointed, Dan assured Mark he would keep him in mind for the following year. Mark hung up the phone and smiled because he had taken an important step toward keeping his circus lineup in order.

A Participant from the Audience

As Mark turned off his office lights and headed toward the stairs (no more elevator rides for him if it was four floors or less), he felt a sense of relief.

With his latest project complete and successfully implemented, he could take a much-needed break. The long weekend would be spent with Lisa and Jackie at a house in the mountains.

"No phones. No deadlines. My focus will definitely be on just two of my rings for the next few days," he thought.

Before reaching the stairway, he saw a light on in Greg's office. Greg was a manager in another department. Knowing that Greg was deep in the throes of a difficult project, he stopped by to lighten the moment with a little clown act.

Greg tried to laugh as Mark delivered his best joke, but stress prevented him from fully enjoying the moment.

"I just can't get my staff to commit more energy to the project," Greg explained. "I know they are overworked, but so am I. What is it they don't get?"

"Have you asked them?" Mark asked.

"Just come out and say, 'What can I do to help you commit?' " Greg retorted.

"Maybe not so forward," Mark replied, "but you have the right idea."

Mark sat down and pulled a piece of paper marked Professional Ring out of his briefcase. On it was drawn a large ring with the name of each member of Mark's department listed inside.

Mark talked with Greg about how he had worked individually with each member of his staff to better meet their needs at a time when he had placed tremendous demands on their time and energy.

For example, he allowed Ben to come into work an hour late so he could help his wife with their new baby. For Susan, who worked in the background, he had written "weekly praise" as a reminder to give positive feedback on her value to the project.

"What's this list under the word 'department' all about?" Greg asked.

"Those are things I did to take care of the team. One weekend, I invited all of the team members and their families to come to my house for dinner. Nothing elaborate, just a chance to get together, laugh and relax. I even printed signs that read 'No work discussions allowed here' to remind them why we were together.

"Another time, I rented a few lanes at the local bowling alley. We took a long lunch and enjoyed relieving our stress by pretending the bowling pins were frustrations."

"These are great ideas, Mark. You're a genius!" Greg replied.

"No, I was a general manager," Mark replied, recalling meeting April during his visit to the circus a few months ago.

"A what?" Greg asked, puzzled.

"Oh, nothing," Mark said.

Intermission

While at lunch one day in a local restaurant, Mark heard someone say, "So, Mark, still attempting your juggling elephants routine?" The voice was unmistakable. A few tables over was Victor.

"My goodness," Mark said. "I saw the signs for the circus and thought of you and Dominic. But don't tell me you're spending your break here again this year. Really, Victor, you need to work on your self ring," Mark joked.

Victor laughed and said, "No, this is the year when my circus tours in this part of the country. So tell me, Mark, how is *your* circus?"

Intermission
is an essential
part of creating
a better circus
performance.

"Very good," Mark replied. "My team and I are more productive at work, and I haven't had a staff member leave in a year. I've lost seventeen pounds and even ran in a 5k for the first time in years. My relationship with Jackie has improved, too."

Victor noticed a touch of caution in Mark's voice.

"Wait a minute. Something is not quite right here," Victor said. "You have all these things going well. You should be on top of the world. What's wrong?"

"Well, to put it in circus terms," Mark confessed, "I feel like the audience is clapping, but I'm not getting any standing ovations. My life is good, but I just know it could be better."

Victor asked, "When was your last intermission?"

"Intermission?" Mark repeated.

"When was the last time you took some time off from your everyday acts?" Victor explained.

"I don't know," Mark replied. "I typically just keep choosing the most important ring to perform in, choose the right act and get to work. Isn't that what you and Dominic taught me?"

"Yes," Victor replied, "but there's more to the circus than the acts in the lineup. **Intermission is an essential part of creating a better circus performance.**"

"Have you ever thought about why there is an intermission at the circus?" Victor asked.

What have you done to improve your performance in one or more of your rings?

"I would imagine it's to give the performers a break," replied Mark.

"That's partially correct," Victor said. "Why would an intermission benefit the audience, as well?"

"Peanuts and hot dogs!" Mark replied with a laugh.

"Cute answer, Mark," said Victor. "But think about it. Intermission is a time for the audience to mentally relax, physically stretch and be better prepared for the second half, whether it's a circus performance or a theatre performance."

Victor continued. "One other point that may be helpful: Who have you invited to be in your audience lately?"

"OK, I have no clue where you are going with this one," Mark said.

Victor replied, "What I mean is, **What have you done to improve your performance in one or more of your rings?** Do you remember my reason for being at the circus last year?"

"I'm not sure I know what you mean," Mark said.

"I was on break when I met you at the circus, but Dominic had asked me to be there," Victor explained. "He wanted me to evaluate his performance and offer feedback."

"But Dominic is such an accomplished ringmaster," Mark said. "Why is feedback important to him?"

Your circus is only as good as your next performance.

"One of Dominic's favorite sayings is, '**Your circus is only as good as your next performance.**' Dominic takes pride in knowing that last night's performance was good, but he wants to make sure that each time he serves as ringmaster, his performance is better than the last. He even asks for feedback from the audience."

"Would all this have anything to do with the people I saw talking with Dominic that day I stopped by the arena?" Mark asked.

"Yes," Victor said. "Those people had been in the audience during the week. They were asked to complete a survey on how the circus was doing as a total unit. Not just the acts, but the concessions, availability of information—anything that affected their experience at the circus."

"Such first-hand information gives us a good idea of our strengths and what we need to focus on improving for our next show or next year," Victor explained. "It all goes back to fulfilling our purpose."

"That seems like an enormous amount of work. Couldn't you just use your own personal evaluations to improve?" Mark asked.

"That's always a good place to start, but sometimes we are too close to really be objective," Victor replied, adding, "We need outside viewpoints from people who will give us honest feedback and even offer solutions, if possible."

"Has Dominic ever visited *your* circus?" Mark asked.

"Sure," Victor said. "Each time, he evaluated something different—the pace of the circus or how the performers interacted with the audience, for example."

"Do you ever have other people watch your circus?" Mark asked.

"Sure," Victor replied, "but not always as formally as in my evaluations from Dominic.

"For example, if I'm struggling with how to best describe an act, I talk with individuals who can help me craft the most effective wording.

"Last year, I attended a conference to learn how to more effectively handle change in my life," Victor recalled. "I picked up several powerful strategies that I still use today. And speaking of time," Victor said, "I hate to cut this short, but tonight is my first performance in your city. I would hate for the local papers to report, 'Acts are great, but ringmaster needs work.' "

"It was good to see you again, Victor," Mark said.

"Same here," Victor replied. "May all…"

Mark stopped him abruptly, "I know… May all your days be circus days!"

Victor laughed and said, "I think you would make a great ringmaster."

"I *am* a great ringmaster," Mark replied, "The ringmaster of my own circus."

Victor smiled in approval.

Change in the Program

As he ate his lunch, Mark reflected on Victor's words. He thought about the idea of an intermission and knew it would be helpful. He had been so busy concentrating on working *in* his life that he had not taken a step back to really look at how he could better work *on* his life.

Inviting people to help improve an area of his life was as exciting as it was scary. It reminded him of his high school coach, who always said, "You can never improve your game unless you play someone better than you."

Mark thought about a conversation he had with a close friend right after Jackie's birth. He and Lisa had always admired her and her husband's relationship with their children.

Juggling Elephants?

While he had not found every idea to be helpful, her insight on parenting techniques had helped him develop a better relationship with Jackie.

"I guess I'll have to find some other ringmasters to watch my circus," he thought. He finished his lunch and returned to work.

Mark kept thinking about the idea of an intermission. "A time when I'm not actively working with my everyday acts. A time to reflect and renew." The idea was tempting, and the opportunity for such an event came sooner than he expected.

Mark had a regional manager's meeting coming up on a Monday and Tuesday at a resort along the coast, and Lisa and Jackie already had plans to visit Lisa's mom for the weekend. Mark decided to drive to the resort on Friday evening and give himself an intermission.

After checking in and having dinner, he took a leisurely jog along the beach. At first, his thoughts turned to work and other things going on in his life, but he quickly reminded himself that the purpose of an intermission was to rest and renew his mental and physical energy.

Mark started focusing on the sound of the waves breaking on the shoreline and the feel of the night air. Doing so relieved much of the tension and anxiety he had been experiencing. He jogged a while longer before retiring to his room.

Mark awoke the next morning a little later than usual; the extra hour of sleep was just what he needed. He got dressed, grabbed his fishing gear from the car and walked to the pier.

The morning sun was hanging over the horizon, and the weather was absolutely perfect. He couldn't remember when he had felt such a sense of renewed energy. The seagulls screeching, the scent of salt air and the gentle breeze were refreshing. While fishing on the pier, he had no time constraints, no ringing phones and no deadlines.

When he packed up his fishing gear a few hours later, Mark realized that thoughts about the acts in the three rings of his life were returning. The intermission, however, had sharpened his focus and renewed his energy, so he welcomed the opportunity to fully engage in thinking about them.

Mark began his Sunday morning by reading the newspaper and enjoying a hot breakfast. After visiting a local church for worship, he took a walk along the beach.

Walking back to his room, Mark thought, "I believe I am ready to take my circus to the next level."

He took out his planning sheets from the past several months and started by simply reviewing the acts that had taken place. Reflecting on them made him smile.

"I have been so busy completing these acts that I haven't taken the time to step into the audience and appreciate the performance," he thought.

Mark turned his attention to the future, starting with his self ring because it was the one most often neglected.

Reviewing his purpose for that ring, Mark listed some acts he would like to see over the next six to twelve months.

Before leaving his self ring, he began lining up the acts and briefly outlining ways to make each one successful. He completed the same process for his relationship ring.

His feeling of clarity about what he wanted to accomplish was energizing and he was excited about getting started on those acts. Once he'd finished his planning with the other two rings, Mark could focus more clearly on his professional ring.

He listed the acts that needed to be performed, then placed them in the lineup. Up next was the director's meeting.

He took extra time on this act, focusing on how he could acquire the skills to more efficiently accomplish the department's goals while engaging the strengths of each department member.

He finished planning, thinking to himself, "If I can make these acts successful in my circus, my boss and I will both be giving it a standing ovation."

The Monday meeting started in the usual way. A light breakfast on the patio was a great opportunity to catch up with other managers.

As much as Mark was ready to focus his energy on the main purpose of the meeting, he knew that this was a time for him to be in his relationship ring as much as it was for him to be in his professional ring. He focused on getting to know the new managers and renewing relationships with the others.

It wasn't long after the meeting started that Mark's intermission and focused planning time began to reveal itself. While some managers wanted to use the time to gripe about past failures, Mark was offering objective insights about both the successes and shortcomings of his department.

In their afternoon brainstorming session, Mark listed two key strategies that he believed would help his department be more successful next year, then asked for feedback.

While some seemed skeptical, everyone was pleasantly surprised when Mark was able to outline how the strategies could be integrated into the company by weaving his initial plan with feedback from the group.

As the meeting ended, a senior vice president shook Mark's hand and said, "Mark, you and I have been coming to these meetings for years. Normally, you show up, make your report and that's about it.

"Today you were different," he continued. "At any point in the meeting, I could see you were fully engaged in what was being discussed. You gave us two really good ideas for the company and led the discussion on how to implement them. My only question is, 'What changed?' "

"Well, let's just say I've spent some time getting my act together," Mark replied, thinking about the value of an intermission.

"Whatever you're doing," he said with a smile, "keep it up. We need more leaders like you in our organization."

"There's one standing ovation already," Mark thought as he headed for his car.

A New Level of Performance

R eturning home, Mark put one of his ideas into action immediately. The very next day at work, he stopped by to see George, the most successful manager in the company. After exchanging some pleasantries, he got down to business.

"George, I know you are busy, but I could really use your help. I have always been impressed with your ability to break a project down into a logical sequence and flow.

"My next project is going to be a nightmare to plan," he explained. "I was wondering if you could give me some tips on how to lay it out?"

George seemed flattered.

"Mark, I would be glad to show you what I know, if you really think it would be helpful," he said.

Mark set up a time to take George to lunch and thanked him for his willingness to help.

During his intermission, Mark had also reflected on the need to begin working on an advanced degree if he wanted to move up in the company. He contacted three friends who had taken a similar career path and asked each of them about their experience and what they would change. The information he gained prevented Mark from making the costly mistake of choosing the wrong degree program or institution.

A personal issue that was on his mind during intermission was a recent conversation with Lisa about having a second child. Mark and Lisa both wanted more children, but with their rings already full, they just didn't know how they would manage the change.

To get some help in this ring, Mark and Lisa talked with dual-career friends who had more than one child. They asked questions such as, "How do you deal with the extra responsibility?" and "How do you find time for each other and the children, while still being able to focus on your jobs?"

Again, their insight was invaluable. Mark and Lisa also took advantage of the opportunity to participate in a retreat to help strengthen their marriage.

Mark took a more proactive approach to his own needs. He started getting regular physical checkups and, for a brief time, even secured the services of a personal trainer. He scheduled time to go fishing, hiking and even to play a round of golf with his friends.

One day while looking for something in his desk drawer, Mark came across the program from the circus he and Jackie had attended almost three years earlier. He smiled as he recalled that first meeting with Victor.

I was just too busy trying to juggle elephants, he thought. Mark vowed to never again forget that he was the ringmaster of his own circus.

After the Story

The Grand Finale

As Mark stepped off the stairs, he wondered if Jackie had finished reading the story. More important, he wondered if she had gotten anything out of it.

"She probably already called Lisa and told her I have a secret fantasy of joining the circus," he thought.

Opening the door to his office, Mark saw Jackie busily writing.

"Still think I'm crazy?" he asked.

"If you are, then put me in the same category," she answered, holding up a sheet of paper.

Mark sat down next to Jackie and looked at the paper. It was strangely familiar.

"What are you doing?" he asked.

"Working on my lineup," Jackie answered.

"Dad, you know how independent I can be. I have always tried to deal with my problems on my own and take pride in being able to work things out.

"When I walked into your office earlier today, I really needed help. The last place I expected to find it was in a recollection of your experience with a circus performance.

"Dad, your story is fantastic," Jackie said. "I can really relate to many of the things you talk about."

"How so?" Mark replied.

"The first idea that really hit home was how the ringmaster has the greatest influence on the success of the circus.

"I had been looking at my situation and feeling like a victim, helpless to change," Jackie recounted. "That part made me realize that if things are to improve, I have to take control rather than let my circumstances control me.

"Now, as I plan the rest of my week in the office, I'm focusing more on what acts *should* be in the ring and how to make them successful. One thing I want to make happen soon is an intermission for the staff."

"Good idea," Mark said.

"It would be so helpful for my team right now," Jackie replied. "We have been so drained lately because of our workload. If we had a few hours together to do something other than focus on our next deadline, it would energize us to be more engaged when we return to work."

"I hope you don't mind, Dad," Jackie said, "But I would like to take your story with me and make copies of it. There are people at work who could use it right now."

"I'm flattered," Mark responded.

Jackie continued. "One person who will definitely get a copy is Blake. He works so hard, but sometimes on the wrong things. By the end of the day, he's frustrated. I think he will really connect with the part of the story about acts serving a purpose."

Jackie laughed and added, "I can see him now, looking at his to do list, marking things off, saying 'This act does not belong in my circus.'

"Another person I might give the story to is Wendy, our vice president of marketing. She has such a passion to see her department succeed. However, her last few productions have not gone very well. The part in the story about the need for acts to begin and end at different times should help her see the need to manage her projects and resources more effectively."

"And the third copy?" Mark asked.

"That's for the next person I meet who is trying to juggle elephants," she answered. "It's so easy to let yourself get overwhelmed trying to get everything done and meet all the expectations you create for yourself... and that others put on you.

"Pretty soon, you either feel like some part of your life is going to crash down like an elephant you actually threw into the air, or you see your situation as impossible.

"The story is a fun way to recognize current challenges and discover practical tools to accomplish what is really important, both at work and in your personal life," Jackie surmised.

Jackie stood up and hugged her dad.

"Speaking of getting things done, I need to start heading home," she said. "I have a feeling, though, that there will be many more circus discussions over the next few months. Thanks for taking me to the circus… again," she said, gesturing with the story in her hand.

"My pleasure," Mark said. "The circus will be back in the spring. Why don't we plan on going again, just you and me. That should really bring the concepts to life. I'll even buy the peanuts."

"You've got a deal," Jackie replied, laughing. "Until then, I'll just let your story be my food for thought."

With another quick hug, Jackie left her dad's office and headed home.

Let the Performance Begin!

Now it's time to get your "act" together!

To learn more about:

- ☑ Ordering copies of *Juggling Elephants?*
- ☑ Keynotes
- ☑ Training
- ☑ Other products or services

Visit: www.jugglingelephants.com

Or call: 1-800-853-4676